REAWAKENING LITERATURE

WORKING WITH CLASSIC LITERATURE RETELLINGS

A GUIDE FOR EDUCATORS

WITHDRAWN FROM STOCK

SOUTH DUBLIN COUNTY LIBRARIES	
SD900000115702	
Bertrams	04/12/2013
	£4.99
	NC

D0257150

www.realreads.co.uk

Jane Campion

Published by Real Reads Ltd
Stroud, Gloucestershire, UK
www.realreads.co.uk

Text copyright © Jane Campion 2013
Illustrations copyright © Real Reads Ltd 2013
The right of Jane Campion to be identified as author of
this book has been asserted by her in accordance with the
Copyright, Design and Patents Act 1988

First published in 2013

All rights reserved
No part of this publication may be reproduced or transmitted in any
form or by any means, electronic or mechanical, including
photocopy, recording, or any information storage and retrieval
system, without permission in writing from the publisher.

ISBN 978-1-906230-73-9

Printed in China by Wai Man Book Binding (China) Ltd
Designed by Lucy Guenot
Typeset by Bookcraft Ltd, Stroud, Gloucestershire

CONTENTS

LUCAN
LIBRARY
TEL. 6216422

INTRODUCTION

Real Reads allow readers of all ages to engage with great stories and begin to explore the wealth of our world's literary heritage. In addition, these accessible texts can be used to support the language and literacy development of primary and secondary students, and people of all ages who are learning English.

Reawakening Literature is intended to support educators in a number of ways to help maximise their students' reading experience. It helps to identify opportunities to develop reading skills, to support talking about books, and to aid the development of the wider cultural and social context of the classical texts.

Reawakening Literature is divided into five essential elements of studying narrative texts:

- plot and structure
- character
- themes and ideas
- looking at language
- the social and historical context in which the text was produced

Each section offers a range of activities suitable for one-to-one tuition, working with small groups, or with whole classes. The activities are designed to encourage the reader's engagement with the text, strengthen comprehension, and support the development of more complex skills such as inferential reading. For each, there is an explanation of the activity with a worked example using one of the **Real Reads** texts. There are also suggestions of other texts for which the activity might work well, and ideas for how the activity might be extended.

ACTIVITY CATEGORIES

Most of the activities in *Reawakening Literature* can be adapted to any learning setting. These recommendations are intended only to give a quick indication of suitability.

 Can be done before starting to read the book

 Can be done after reading only part of the book

 Can be done when the whole book has been read

 Suitable for one-to-one tuition

 Suitable for a small group of students

 Suitable for a whole class

PLOT AND STRUCTURE

Engaging with a brilliant plot is the hook that catches the reader. Whether it is full of twists and turns, a murder mystery or a romance, literature is characterised by compelling and timeless plots. Students need to

- get to grips with the plot of the novel
- learn to analyse its structure
- identify the significant events that shape the story
- recognise how characters' interactions affect the course of the story
- understand how writers vary the pace to keep us engaged

PREDICTING THE PLOT

Students can make predictions based on illustrations from the book or a reading of the first page before reading the whole book. This encourages students to continue reading to verify their predictions.

Dr Jekyll and Mr Hyde (Stevenson)

Try giving students a selection of pictures in sequence and asking them to predict what the story will be.

Extend by muddling up the pictures and asking students to sequence them as they make their predictions. Words or phrases from the text can be added to the pictures.

Hyde's rooms were a mess.

Other suitable **Real Reads** texts include

The Murders in the Rue Morgue
(Poe)   Use the *Gazette des Tribunaux* article on pages 18 and 19 of the **Real Reads** version as a starting point.

Romeo and Juliet
(Shakespeare)   Provide details about the feud between the Montagues and Capulets to get students started.

PICTURING THE SETTING

In some stories, the setting is crucial to the power of the tale. Helping students to visualise it can bring the story alive for them.

Far from the Madding Crowd (Hardy)

Try finding pictures on the internet of Dorchester (Casterbridge in the novel) and other places in Dorset, England, where the story might have taken place.

Other suitable **Real Reads** texts include

Pride and Prejudice (Austen)   Find pictures of grand houses such as the one Mr Darcy lives in.

Wuthering Heights (Brontë)   Find pictures of places in Yorkshire that Emily Brontë would have known, such as Haworth and the Pennine Hills.

The Old Curiosity Shop and *Hard Times* (Dickens)   Find pictures of mid-Victorian industrial cities like London and Manchester.

TRACKING THE ACTION

Activities that help students to visualise the storyline can help them to understand the action, particularly where the plot is complex. Where the action of the story moves geographically, it can help to track the journey on a map.

The Three Kingdoms (Guanzhong)

Try enlarging the map in the book and identifying the locations of some of the events of the story.

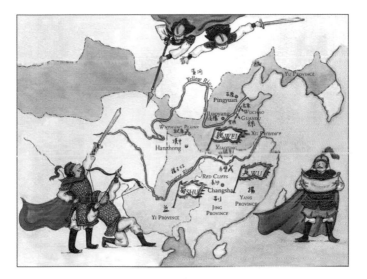

Extend by linking the locations to illustrations, descriptions and other details from the book.

Other suitable **Real Reads** texts include

War of the Worlds **(Wells)**   Use a map of South London and Surrey (southern England) to track the narrator's journey.

The Odyssey **(Homer)**   Create a map of the places Odysseus visits, including Troy, the cave of Cyclops, the island of the Sirens, the Scylla's lair, and Ithaca. Some are real places; others can only be guessed at.

Paul of Tarsus   Use the map in the 'Taking things further' section to trace Paul's journeys.

MAPPING THE STORY

Creating graphics such as maps, diagrams, storyboards and flowcharts can help those who struggle with written language.

***Macbeth* (Shakespeare)**

Try completing a simple story map as you read the play, dividing the action into a beginning, a middle and an end.

Extend by creating a more complex story map where the action is divided into five or six stages.

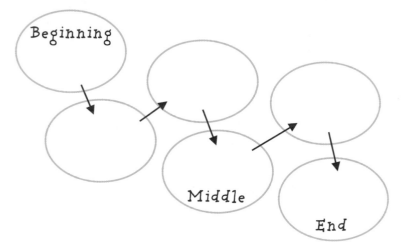

Students can also turn their descriptive map into a storyboard with pictures.

TRACING THE TENSION

Readers are gripped by moments of tension in a story. Tracing the way tension builds can help students appreciate the writer's technique, as well as giving them a more detailed insight into the way stories are shaped.

The Hound of the Baskervilles (Conan Doyle)

Try drawing a graph to plot the fluctuating tension as the plot develops. Keywords, illustrations and descriptions can be added to develop a more detailed picture.

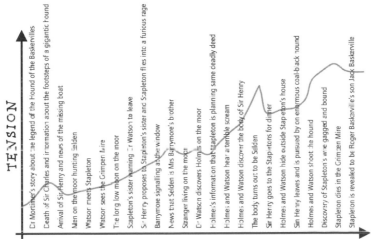

Extend by honing the focus and looking at how tension is built at paragraph and sentence level.

Other suitable **Real Reads** texts include

The Iliad (Homer)   **The Moonstone (Collins)**

SEQUENCING EVENTS

Using words and pictures to organise the events in a story can help to reinforce a student's knowledge of that story and is also a useful way of checking understanding.

Waverley (Scott)

Try selecting keywords and pictures to label each significant event in the story.

Extend by muddling up these keywords and pictures; challenge students to match the words to pictures and then sequence them.

loch
battle cry
gravel
royal highness
cave
armed men
pretty
impaled
boat
girl
pike

Other suitable **Real Reads** texts include

The Time Machine (Wells)   ***Huckleberry Finn*** (Twain)

FREEZE-FRAMES

Getting physically active is a great way of reinforcing a plot, and can help reluctant students engage with a text.

Journey to the West (Cheng'en)

Try breaking the plot down into several stages. Ask students to create a tableau for each stage, perhaps using props and even improvised costumes.

Extend by breaking the story down into more stages. Ask students to set the tableaux to a suitable piece of music that represents the mood or a theme of the story.

Other suitable **Real Reads** texts include

Dr Jekyll and Mr Hyde (Stevenson)

The Mill on the Floss (Eliot)   *Rob Roy* (Scott)

REFERRING TO THE ORIGINAL

The 'Filling in the spaces' section at the back of the books can be used to explore some of the omitted scenes in their original form, or as inspiration for creative writing.

A Christmas Carol (Dickens)

Try asking pupils to role play an omitted scene, such as people talking about Scrooge's funeral. What would they say? How would they feel? Pupils could also role-play Scrooge's response to hearing what they say.

Extend by finding the scene in the original book. Use this as a stimulus for creative writing. Pupils could retell this scene for themselves, aiming to borrow some of Dickens' language. This scene in the original version is given in context opposite.

The spirit stopped beside one little knot of business men. Observing that the hand was pointed to them, Scrooge advanced to listen to their talk.

'No,' said a great fat man with a monstrous chin, 'I don't know much about it, either way. I only know he's dead.'

'When did he die?' enquired another.

'Last night, I believe.'

'Why, what was the matter with him?' asked a third, taking a vast quantity of snuff out of a very large snuff box. 'I thought he'd never die.'

'God knows,' said the first, with a yawn.

'What has he done with his money?' asked a red-faced gentleman with a pendulous excrescence on the end of his nose, that shook like the gills of a turkey-cock.

'I haven't heard,' said the man with the large chin, yawning again. 'Left it to his company, perhaps. He hasn't left it to me. That's all I know.'

This pleasantry was received with a general laugh.

'It's likely to be a very cheap funeral,' said the same speaker; 'for upon my life I don't know of anybody to go to it. Suppose we make up a party and volunteer?'

'I don't mind going if a lunch is provided,' observed the gentleman with the excrescence on his nose. 'But I must be fed, if I make one!'

Another laugh.

'Well, I am the most disinterested among you, after all,' said the first speaker, 'for I never wear black gloves, and I never eat lunch. But I'll offer

49

Other suitable **Real Reads** texts include

Far from the Madding Crowd **(Hardy)**   Use the scene of Gabriel and Bathsheba's marriage.

Mansfield Park **(Austen)**   Use a scene where Fanny returns to her family in Portsmouth.

CHARACTER

Getting to know the characters is one of the joys of reading a novel. Often in the classics, the characters have timeless qualities that help readers down the ages to identify and relate to them.

● Students can be engaged in stories by acquiring a detailed knowledge of their characters – identifying their characteristics, considering their qualities, putting themselves in the characters' shoes.

● Work on characters can be a good introductory activity to encourage students to start reading the story.

MIX AND MATCH

Use the 'Characters' pages of the story to get the students reading and thinking.

Oliver Twist (Dickens)

Try separating the illustrations from the character descriptions and asking students to match the pictures to the text, justifying their choices.

Mr Brownlow is a respectable and warm-hearted old gentleman. Can his fondness for Oliver overcome distrust and doubt?

Fagin looks after orphaned boys, as long as they earn him money. Can he make himself rich by turning Oliver into a thief?

Nancy works for Fagin and loves Bill Sikes; she has a warm heart. Can she save Oliver?

Oliver is an orphan. Is he strong enough to resist Fagin's attempts to make him a thief?

Bill Sikes is a hardened criminal who works with Fagin. Can he control Nancy and still keep her love? Will he ruin Oliver?

Try distributing the illustrations among a group, and put the descriptions, with names removed, in the middle. Students match their illustration with the correct description. In pairs, they then discuss how their respective characters might act in the story.

Extend by asking students to infer aspects of the characters. Students might try and work out who is good and who is bad. Remind them that they might revise their choices as they read the novel.

Other suitable **Real Reads** texts include

***Sense and Sensibility* (Austen)**   Discuss how easy it is to judge from the look of the young men and women which character description fits each best.

***Twelfth Night* (Shakespeare)**   Pupils will need to take account of Viola's double identity.

BECOME AN ILLUSTRATOR

Students can engage imaginatively with characters by using descriptions in the text as a starting point for their own drawings.

Great Expectations (Dickens)

Try using the passage below as the basis for an illustration. Colour is important in the description, so make sure the students think about the colours they are choosing. They could underline all the words that suggest colour (or its absence), and discuss what they can infer about Miss Havisham.

> Miss Havisham, like a ghost, was a vision of paleness. She wore a long, faded white dress of satin and lace, with white shoes of the same material. Her skin and hair had faded almost to white, and from her white hair hung a faded white veil. Even the flowers in her hair, which must once have been so colourful, had faded to colourless white. The only relief amidst all this lost beauty was provided by her sparkling diamond necklace.

Extend by asking what the character's history might be and how it might have affected his or her character. For Miss Havisham, students might notice that her portrait in the book resembles a bride, so the obvious question is 'What happened on her wedding day?'

Other suitable **Real Reads** texts include

A Christmas Carol **(Dickens)**   Use the Ghost of Christmas Present.

Dr Jekyll and Mr Hyde **(Stevenson)**   Use the description of Henry Jekyll's transformation into Edward Hyde.

RELATIONSHIPS

As students are reading a book, it is important that they notice how characters develop over time as a result of people they meet and things that happen to them. The main character's relationships with other characters often provide the focus for the plot and its development. Students can locate key moments in the development of a relationship that help to reveal and shape the character.

The Mayor of Casterbridge (Hardy)

Try representing Michael Henchard's relationship with Donald Farfrae as a chart, diagram or mind-map and then describing what we learn about Henchard's character and how this has affected him.

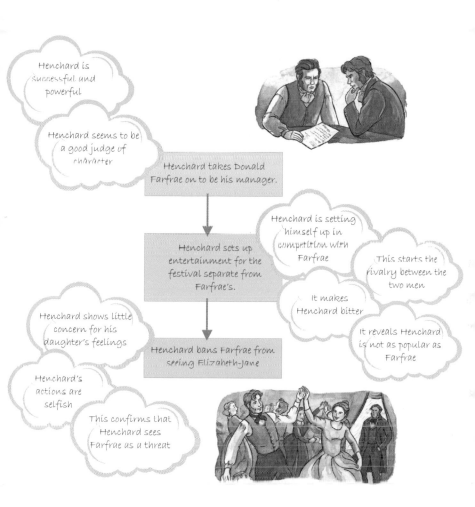

Henchard is successful and powerful

Henchard seems to be a good judge of character

Henchard takes Donald Farfrae on to be his manager.

Henchard is setting himself up in competition with Farfrae

This starts the rivalry between the two men

Henchard sets up entertainment for the festival separate from Farfrae's.

It makes Henchard bitter

Henchard shows little concern for his daughter's feelings

It reveals Henchard is not as popular as Farfrae

Henchard bans Farfrae from seeing Elizabeth-Jane

Henchard's actions are selfish

This confirms that Henchard sees Farfrae as a threat

Other suitable **Real Reads** texts include

Wuthering Heights (Emily Brontë)   Look at the characters of Edgar and Heathcliff.

Pride and Prejudice (Jane Austen)   Look at the characters of Bingley and Darcy.

GETTING INVOLVED

Recreated artefacts from a story can intrigue and engage students and provide a focus for discussion.

The Mayor of Casterbridge (Hardy)

Try giving students a post-dated letter like Susan's letter to Michael Henchard. Do they open it? What do they think about when they are making that decision? What does it say about them if they do open it, or if they don't?

My dear Michael,

I have kept one thing a secret till now. I hope you will understand why. I can hardly write it, but I must. Elizabeth-Jane is not your Elizabeth-Jane. She died after three months. This one is Richard Newson's. I named her the same to heal my loss.

I am dying. Please tell her husband, as you judge. Forgive a woman who you deeply wronged, as she forgives you.

Susan Henchard

Henchard finds Susan's letter which is not to be opened until Elizabeth-Jane's wedding day. Does he open it?

Yes
What might he read there?
What would it show about how he feels about Susan?
How could it affect his relationship with Elizabeth-Jane?

No
What would this say about Henchard's character?
What would it show about how he feels about Susan and Elizabeth-Jane?

Extend by exploring the choices the character from the story might make. Students can consider the consequences of those choices on the character and on their relationships with other characters.

Other suitable **Real Reads** texts include

Emma **(Austen)** Ask students to respond to the letters that Jane sends to her sister Cassandra.

IN THEIR SHOES

Putting the students in the position of a character is a good way to develop empathy.

Mansfield Park (Austen)

Try asking students to take on the part of Fanny Price and write a letter to an agony aunt about her feelings for Edmund. Another student could write the reply.

Extend by asking students to conduct a conversation in which they take the part of different characters in the novel. They might discuss what they think Fanny should do if and when Henry proposes to her.

Other suitable **Real Reads** texts include

***The Woman in White* (Collins)**   Imagine what it would be like to be Laura Fairlie.

***All Quiet on the Western Front* (Remarque)**   Imagine what it would be like to be Paul Bäumer.

WHAT ARE THEY REALLY LIKE?

Often authors don't tell us what characters are really like, but leave us to make inferences and deductions. Developing these skills is important if students are to access more than surface meanings of texts.

By examining the evidence and making their own judgements from the way the characters are described, students can develop these skills.

Tess of the d'Urbervilles (Hardy)

Try examining a significant line in the text. For example, with the lines below students could ask themselves the following questions: Is Tess to blame for what happens to her? Who is to blame for her downfall? Does the student feel sympathy for Tess?

'wondered' shows Tess is thinking hard about what to do

'make amends' shows that Tess feels it is her responsibility to make up for Prince's death

Tess wondered what she could ever do to make amends (page 14)

'her past' shows that Tess cannot get away from what Alec did to her

'could not be true to herself' shows that she is a moral person who intends to do good

'ever do' suggests she thinks it will be very hard or impossible

She knew that she could not be true to herself and her love for him without being completely honest about her past (page 35)

'without being completely honest' shows that she wants her love for Angel Clare to be pure

Extend by making case files for Alec d'Urberville and Angel Clare. Students debate which character is more or less to blame for Tess's downfall using evidence from the text to support their case.

Alec d'Urberville

Evidence	Comment
He has a 'curly moustache', 'swarthy skin', and a 'proud air'.	He has the 'classic' characteristics of a villain.
He 'didn't tell her the truth about his name'.	He is not honest, and therefore not to be trusted.
He always goes 'downhill at full gallop'.	He is reckless and careless with lives – his own and Tess's.
He 'persuaded himself that peasant girls have no minds of their own'.	He has no respect for Tess, and refuses to take responsibility for the effect he might have on her.
'I did wrong to love you when you didn't want me, I admit it.'	He is capable of taking a moral stance.
'I'll pay for my wickedness – as much as you want.'	He believes he can pay compensation for what he has done. He does not realise that money cannot make up for his crime.

Angel Clare

Evidence	Comment
His 'distinctive' appearance 'sets him apart'.	He is presented as out of the ordinary and exceptional.
'He was touched by the innocence and purity he saw in her.' 'She is the purest thing I have ever known.'	He focuses on the idea of her purity, which for him equates with innocence.
'He had her fixed in his mind in a particular way, and could not imagine any other.'	He is inflexible, and thinks he has a clear idea of what and who Tess is. She is the Tess of his imagination.
'You're a different person from the Tess I knew.'	He finds it hard to accept the 'real' Tess.
'When his friend reproached Angel for his behaviour towards Tess, Angel began to realise how wrong he had been.'	It takes someone else to point out Angel's own failings.
'It is my fault – all my fault,' grieved Angel.	He expresses genuine remorse – his grief demonstrates the sense of loss he feels.
'He wished – how he wished – that he could take everything back, begin again.'	The repetition reinforces the sense that he regrets his own part in Tess's downfall.
'He held her hand, waiting, until the warm sun rose and shone upon her body, waking her.'	This touching scene demonstrates that he can be caring.

Other suitable **Real Reads** texts include

Hamlet **(Shakespeare)**   Trace Hamlet's downfall. Examine the speeches of Hamlet, Claudius, the ghost of Hamlet's father and Gertrude to explore who is responsible for the tragedy.

HEROES, HEROINES AND OTHERS

Protagonists in classical literature often fill archetypal roles such as 'hero', 'lover' or 'villain'. An exploration of a character's qualities can help students discover how such roles have been perceived over time. It can also help students to empathise with different characters and assess their own allegiances.

Jane Eyre (Charlotte Brontë)

Try mind-mapping Jane's contrasting characteristics, attaching quotations from the novel to justify the descriptions. How do we view these qualities today?

Extend by evaluating her character. Is she an admirable character? Is she a likeable character? How independent is she? What in the story constrains her and how might things be different for her today?

'I teased him and kept him cross and crusty'
'restlessness was, and still is, in my nature'
'I longed for more'
'yearned for liberty'
'I fled, without money or possessions'

PATIENT
'suppress a sob'
'my tears subsided'

INDEPENDENT

DEPENDENT
'no longer his shadow's prisoner, I was
thoroughly alive'
'I was no longer alone'
'Reader, I married him'

PASSIONATE
'I burned inside'
'failed to cool my fire'
'hot tears of anger and
humiliation'
'burst into volcanic revolt'
'I grieved for him'

WEAK
'I submitted to St John'
'I wept'
'I sank, weeping on the doorstep'

FRIENDLY
'the other girls accepted me'
'I put my arms around my
friend's neck'
'Aunt, you have my full
forgiveness'

STRONG
'I made good progress in my studies'
'I will not leave you, sir'
'I succeeded in extinguishing the fire'
'bore my punishment because I had to'
'filled with energy and resolve'

HOSTILE
'I will never call you aunt again'
'I scorn your cold idea of marriage'

Other suitable **Real Reads** texts include

The Old Curiosity Shop (Dickens)   Look at the plight of Nell.

The Riddle of the Sands (Childers)   Look at the qualities of Carruthers.

The Mill on the Floss (Eliot)   Look at the qualities of Maggie.

THEMES AND IDEAS

Literary texts are generally more than just a good story. Often writers are commenting on, or criticising, a particular aspect of society or human behaviour. Sometimes writers want to make us think about people's motivations or reactions to particular and extreme situations; sometimes they want to explore aspects of morality and the nature of good and evil; and sometimes they want to contemplate the nature of our very existence and how we came to be. Explorations of the wider significance of literature can help students' personal and social development as well as broaden their understanding and appreciation of their own and others' cultural heritage.

CUTTING AND STICKING

Visual representations of abstract ideas and emotions can help students relate such ideas to concrete objects and experiences.

Wuthering Heights (Emily Brontë)

Try collecting words and pictures from newspapers and magazines to create a collage representing the relationship between Cathy and Heathcliff.

Extend by dividing up the collage to represent different thematic elements, such as love, passion, revenge, social class, nature, the supernatural.

Other suitable **Real Reads** texts include

Persuasion (Austen)   Look at the love between Anne and Captain Wentworth.

Great Expectations (Dickens)   Look at Pip as a gentleman.

Waverley (Scott)   Look at Edward's divided loyalties.

PLAYING THE PART

Where texts explore different aspects of human behaviour, role play can be an invaluable way of understanding a character's responses and relating them to real-life situations.

Silas Marner (Eliot)

Try acting out different parts of the novel where Silas is misunderstood or shunned. Talk about how this might feel.

Extend by identifying real situations in which people are cast out from society as a result of their appearance.

Other suitable **Real Reads** texts include

Dr Jekyll and Mr Hyde (Stevenson)   Act out the transformation from the upright and respectable Dr Jekyll to the savage Mr Hyde.

Frankenstein (Shelley)   Act out different episodes in the novel when the monster is rejected.

MORAL DILEMMAS

Often, the rights or wrongs of a situation are not clear. Trying to weigh up the relative virtues of protagonists can help students engage with the complexities of making decisions as well as understand how moral frameworks might shift over time.

The Sign of the Four (Conan Doyle)

Try placing some of the key characters in the novel on a scale of virtue to vice using pictures.

Extend by adding details of the characters' actions and motivations.

Other suitable **Real Reads** texts include

The Tempest (Shakespeare)   Consider the rights and wrongs of Caliban's, Prospero's and Ariel's actions.

Ramayana (Valmiki)   Weigh up the relative vices and virtues of Ravana and Rama.

FATE OR FREE WILL?

From the ancient legends through Shakespeare to more recent novels, writers have explored the way in which humans sometimes appear to be subject to things beyond their control. Discussing how far characters are responsible for their own fate can prove a lively way to engage students in some of the big questions as well as developing their speaking and listening skills.

Romeo and Juliet (Shakespeare)

Try debating who or what is responsible for the tragedy of the play.

Extend by challenging students to find evidence in the text to support their arguments.

Other suitable **Real Reads** texts include

The Mill on the Floss (Eliot) What role does 'fate' play in Maggie's tragedy?

The Odyssey (Homer) How far is Odysseus responsible for his own successes and failures? How much can the gods be held responsible for what happens to him?

A Midsummer Night's Dream (Shakespeare) How much do Oberon and Puck influence the lovers?

TRACING THE THEME

Students sometimes find it difficult to distinguish between the plot and the theme of a story. Activities that draw a distinction between these two aspects of a text – what actually happens and the ideas that are being explored – can help.

Macbeth (Shakespeare)

Try creating a theme web by identifying the three apparitions in *Macbeth* and connecting them with the different themes in the play.

Extend by using the information in the web to explain the ways in which Shakespeare uses the apparitions to explore the play's main themes.

Other suitable **Real Reads** texts include

Northanger Abbey (Austen)   Look at all the references to novels. What is Jane Austen suggesting about novels and the readers of them?

Huckleberry Finn (Twain)   Look at all the references to the river and travelling. What is Mark Twain saying about Huck and his journey?

Theme 1
power and ambition

Second apparition
Be bloody, bold, and resolute;
laugh to scorn
The power of man, for none
of woman born
Shall harm Macbeth.

First apparition
Macbeth, Macbeth, Macbeth.
Beware Macduff, beware the
Thane of Fife.

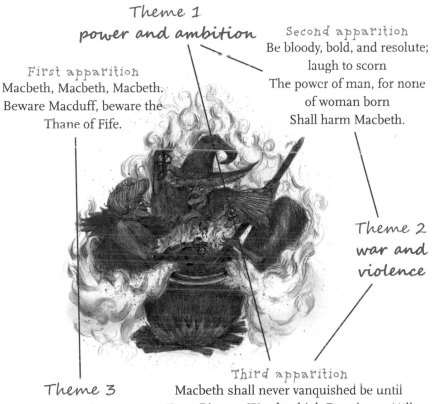

Theme 2
war and
violence

Theme 3
kingship
and tyranny

Third apparition
Macbeth shall never vanquished be until
Great Birnam Wood to high Dunsinane Hill
Shall come against him.

COMPARING TEXTS

Sometimes looking at two or more texts together can be more revealing than looking at them separately. The elements that they have in common can help students define some of the characteristics of particular genres too.

Midsummer Night's Dream and *Twelfth Night* (Shakespeare)

Try creating a Venn diagram showing the way in which love is presented in the two plays.

Extend by further comparing these two plays with Shakespeare's later play, *The Tempest*.

Twelfth Night

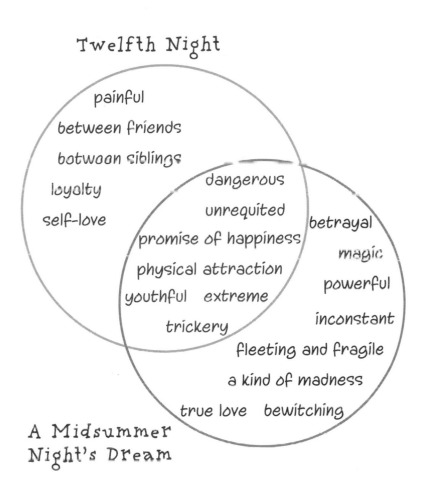

painful

between friends

botwoon siblings

loyalty

self-love

dangerous

unrequited

promise of happiness

physical attraction

youthful   extreme

trickery

betrayal

magic

powerful

inconstant

fleeting and fragile

a kind of madness

true love   bewitching

A Midsummer Night's Dream

Other suitable **Real Reads** texts include

Macbeth and Hamlet (Shakespeare)   Look at the theme of power.

Pride and Prejudice and Persuasion (Austen)   Look at the theme of marriage.

LANGUAGE

Exploring classic literature can aid students' language development and their evolving literacy. It is not only the acquisition of vocabulary that matters, although fluency and precision of expression is important. It is also crucial for students to develop the ability to understand implied as well as literal meanings. More than that, though – if students can identify patterns of language, the way symbols and images combine to create mood and atmosphere, the way a character is invented through patterns of speech, then they can begin to relish the language of literature.

VOCABULARY ENRICHMENT

Much of the language used by writers of the **Real Reads** stories derives from the original text. Helping students to get to grips with difficult vocabulary can help build their reading confidence, and inspire them to tackle the original.

Dracula (Stoker)

Try a dictionary challenge for words from one of Jonathan Harker's diary entries (the flipchart opposite shows words from the entry for 9th August). Divide groups and classes into teams and make it a race.

tempest   immense
bows   beached
            log records
      rosary
stowaway   mastiff
            entire
speculation   cargo
      shore   glimpses
      mirage   lashed

41

Extend by offering students a range of possible meanings. Students can use their knowledge about language to help determine which is the correct meaning. With groups and classes, turn it into a game of 'Call My Bluff' where teams read out two false definitions and one correct definition and the opposing team must decide which is the correct one. Students might also be given the word in its context to help work out what the meaning might be.

Other suitable **Real Reads** texts include

The Hunchback of Notre Dame **(Hugo)**   Include words and phrases like mystery play, hideous sore, multitude, nobility, contestant.

The Woman in White **(Collins)**   Include words and phrases like parish clerk, marriage register, leather-bound, inherit, vestry.

WORD CHOICES

Careful consideration of the words writers
choose can help students appreciate the effects
that language can achieve. Activities that focus
on individual words can also improve students'
reading and writing skills

Dr Jekyll and Mr Hyde (Stevenson)

Try a cloze exercise on the following extract from
page 12 of the Real Reads retelling. Students
choose words to fill the gaps, considering the
different effects achieved by their choices.

He heard footsteps .... down the street.
Utterson .... into a shop doorway
and .... A man appeared out of the
.... into the small .... of gaslight,
reached into his pocket, and produced a key.
He was .... almost .... – and
.... dressed, his face .... by the
brim of his hat. Although he glanced ....
from .... to .... , he failed to spot
Utterson until he was across the street and almost
at the door of the house.

Extend by asking students deliberately to choose
other words to fill the gaps in order to create a
different atmosphere.

FIGURATIVE LANGUAGE

One of the joys of classic texts is the richness of the figurative language. Understanding the way in which writers use language symbolically helps students to become more sophisticated readers who are able to engage with a text on a metaphorical as well as a literal level.

Motifs are recurring elements that appear throughout a narrative. Tracing motifs can help students to track how characters, relationships, moods or fortunes change across the course of a story.

Hard Times (Dickens)

Try collecting all of the images of rock and stone associated with Mr Gradgrind. Discuss the characteristics of rock and stone. What do these characteristics suggest about the character of Gradgrind?

Stone Lodge

Like two great blocks of granite

chiselling at his granite exterior

His voice cracking as the granite crumbled

the ground on which I stand is no longer solid

44

Extend by creating new metaphors or similes for Mr Gradgrind using similar vocabulary, such as rock, grit, gravel, brick, stony.

Or explore some of the other ways that Gradgrind is described. For example, what do the following choices of words suggest about him? What do these have in common with the rock and stone images?

his inflexible, dry tone

his square body

His fingers were all square

His mouth rarely deviated from a perfect straight line

Other suitable **Real Reads** texts include

Oliver Twist **(Dickens)**   Look for images used to describe the different worlds that Oliver inhabits – the dark dingy foggy world of Fagin and the bright sunlit world of Mr Brownlow and Mrs Maylie.

Jane Eyre **(Charlotte Brontë)**   Look at the treatment of Jane by her aunt and Mr Brocklehurst, by Miss Temple and Helen, by Mr Rochester and by St John Rivers.

COMPARISONS

Writers can say a lot about a character or a setting using comparisons. Exploring the implications of metaphors, similes and personification can help students engage with the complexity of a text and start to appreciate the range of meanings a writer can convey.

The Lost World (Conan Doyle)

Try creating drawings of the comparative elements in these examples, and annotating their characteristics.

- Professor Challenger's 'spade-like beard'.

- 'I saw leathery wings, a long snake-like neck.'

- Indians 'as lithe as cats'.

Extend by creating new comparisons to represent the characteristics of different characters in the novel. Students could use the book's illustrations, such as the one opposite from page 24 of the Real Reads retelling, to provide inspiration.

Other suitable **Real Reads** texts include

***The War of the Worlds* (Wells)**   Look at the descriptions of the Martians.

***Macbeth* (Shakespeare)**   Look at Shakespeare's use of extended metaphor, for example, 'that is a step on which I must fall down, or else o'erleap' (page 15 of the **Real Reads** version).

SOUND EFFECTS

Writers use several techniques to create pace
and rhythm and enhance description, including
onomatopoeia, alliteration, assonance and
consonance. Understanding these effects can help
students to develop the descriptive qualities of
their own writing.

Alliteration links the
face with the feelings
to show how visible
David's emotions are.

'Oh, pray don't beat me, sir!' cried David. 'I
do try to be good! I only wanted to talk to my
mother. Oh please!'

David felt that the beating would never
end. He was torn and bleeding, his face red
with fury and fear. Whack! The pain was
unbearable. Whack! He had to act quickly.
Whack! Turning his head, he desperately sank
his teeth deep into Murdstone's arm.

The inevitable punishment followed. The
room in which Murdstone locked David was
dark and dusty. For five
days David sat alone,
longing to weep in
his mother's arms. His
only visitor was
Peggotty, who
delivered his
daily rations of bread
and water.

The repeated
onomatopoeia
echoes the rhythm
of the beating
and punctuates
the description,
emphasising the
shock.

The alliteration
draws attention to
the gloominess of
the room in which
David is locked.

12

48

David Copperfield (Dickens)

Try identifying the different techniques in the passage opposite.

Alliteration is the repetition of the same sound at the beginning of nearby words; onomatopoeia is the use of words that imitate the sounds of the objects or actions to which they refer.

Extend by explaining the effect that each of these techniques has on the reader. What do they help us to understand about David's situation?

Or look at the original text for more uses of such techniques.

Other suitable **Real Reads** texts include

Oliver Twist (Dickens)
Look at the chase scene after the Artful Dodger has stolen from Mr Brownlow.

The Hound of the Baskervilles (Conan Doyle)
Look at the description of the hound on page 46 of the **Real Reads** version.

IMPLIED MEANINGS

READING BETWEEN THE LINES

Reading is about more than recognising and comprehending the words on the page. It is also about detecting and inferring meaning. Learning to read between the lines is an important part of becoming a mature and sophisticated reader.

Emma (Austen)

Try identifying what Emma thinks that Mr Elton feels about Harriet from what he says.

'You have added qualities that nature did not provide.'

'You have passed many of your own fine qualities on to your friend.'

'Let me encourage you, Miss Woodhouse, to exercise your talent in honour of your friend.'

Extend by inferring what Mr Elton really feels about Emma.

Other suitable **Real Reads** texts include

Northanger Abbey (Austen)   What does the narrator really think of Isabella Thorpe's character and how does she convey this (look, for example, at pages 12 and 13 of the **Real Reads** retelling)?

Persuasion (Austen)   What kind of man is Sir Walter Elliot? Notice how the author does not tell us directly about his faults, but demonstrates them through his speech and his actions.

MOOD AND ATMOSPHERE

Some writers create an atmosphere that is really memorable. Gothic tales in particular are characterised by their mysterious mood. An exploration of the words and images that make up the mood and atmosphere can further develop students' appreciation of how language can be used to create an effect.

Frankenstein (Stoker)

Try selecting and sorting the contrasting images into those relating to darkness and those relating to light.

> darker powers
> stormy November night
> moon hid behind a cloud
> dark winter months

> spark of life
> summer walks in the mountains
> flash of lightning
> snow-capped mountains

Extend by creating word walls to reflect moods and atmospheres at different points of the novel. This can help students to identify patterns of language across a whole text.

Other suitable **Real Reads** texts include

The Woman in White (Collins)   Use the contrasting descriptions of Limmeridge House and Blackwater Park.

INSIDE AND OUTSIDE

Writers often use the weather and features of the landscape to underline the feelings of the characters. This technique is known as the pathetic fallacy, and is a form of personification. Sometimes writers use it to reflect or magnify a character's response; sometimes they use it to foreshadow an event that is to come.

Wuthering Heights (Emily Brontë)

Try finding descriptions of different kinds of weather described in the novel and linking them to the feelings of different characters.

Other suitable **Real Reads** texts include

Far from the Madding Crowd (Hardy)

The Hound of the Baskervilles (Conan Doyle)

THE LANGUAGE OF
THE ORIGINALS

At the heart of every **Real Read** is an original text. To give students the confidence to try reading some of the original, they need to be familiar with the language, so the challenge of comprehension does not outweigh the enjoyment of the story.

Hamlet (Shakespeare)

Try exploring the central debate at the heart of Hamlet's famous soliloquies in the **Real Reads** retelling – 'Oh, that this too too solid flesh would melt' (Act 1, Scene 1) and 'To be or not to be' (Act 2, Scene 3). Use a gloss or dictionary to explain unfamiliar words. Students could draw pictures to represent the way in which life and death are characterised.

Hamlet
Oh, that this too too solid flesh would melt,
Thaw, and resolve itself into a dew,
Or that the great almighty had not fixed
His laws against self-slaughter. O god, god,
How weary, stale, flat and unprofitable
Seems to me all the uses of this world!
'Tis but an unweeded garden grown to seed.

The Real Reads
retellings

Hamlet
To be, or not to be; that is the question:
Whether 'tis better to suffer the pain
That life may bring, or else to end it all.
To die, to sleep, perchance to dream, ah me.
But in that sleep of death, what dreams may come
When we have shuffled off this mortal coil?
But soft, the fair Ophelia!

HAMLET

To be, or not to be, — that is the question: —
Whether 'tis nobler in the mind to suffer
The slings and arrows of outrageous fortune,
Or to take arms against a sea of troubles,
And by opposing end them? — To die — to sleep,
No more; and by a sleep to say we end
The heart-ache, and the thousand natural shocks
That flesh is heir to, 'tis a consummation
Devoutly to be wish'd. To die — to sleep; —
To sleep! perchance to dream: ay, there's the rub
For in that sleep of death what dreams may com[e]
When we have shuffled off this mortal coil,
Must give us pause: there's the respect
That makes calamity of so long life;
For who would bear the whips and scorns of tim[e]
The oppressor's wrong, the proud man's contu[mely]
The pangs of despised love, the law's delay,
The insolence of office, and the spurns
That patient merit of the unworthy takes,
When he himself might his quietus make
With a bare bodkin? who would fardels bear,
To grunt and sweat under a weary life,
But that the dread of something after death, —
The undiscover'd country, from whose bourn
No traveller returns,   puzzles the will,
And makes us rather bear those ills we have
Than fly to others that we know not of?

Extend by reading more of the original Shakespeare and adding to the images associated with life and death.

Other suitable **Real Reads** texts include

Bleak House (Dickens)   Use the famous opening of the novel.

Pride and Prejudice (Austen)   Use the encounter in the Bennet's garden between Lady Catherine de Bourgh and Elizabeth.

CONTEXT

Stories inevitably reflect aspects of the time and place in which they were written. Understanding stories as part of a geographical, historical and social context can broaden students' appreciation of people's lives at different times and in different places. In addition, some knowledge about the author can help shed light on the reasons why a writer might have written a particular story.

Literary texts are also part of a particular tradition, and some sense of their place in a literary evolution can shed light on aspects of form and style. It is important to be aware too that texts aren't always just stories. Some texts also have important religious significance, and both represent and shape the identity and beliefs of a particular faith.

GEOGRAPHICAL CONTEXT
MAKING MAPS

Some stories are so rooted in the place from whence they derive that some understanding of the country can really aid comprehension.

Mahabharata (all three volumes)

Try marking on a map of India the significant places cited in the 'Taking things further' section at the back of the books.

Extend by attaching characters and their movements to the map.

Other suitable **Real Reads** texts include

Judas Iscariot and *Paul of Tarsus*   Look at the maps provided and compare it with a modern map.

The Riddle of the Sands (Childers)   Look at the maps provided and find those places on a modern map.

Dracula (Stoker)   Look in the main text as well as the 'Taking things further' section.

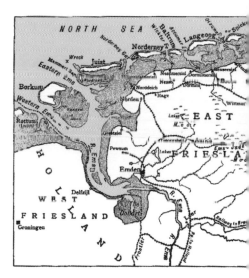

GEOGRAPHICAL CONTEXT
DIALECT WORDS AND IDIOMS

Huckleberry Finn (Twain)

Try decoding the dialect words in the characters' speech. Encourage students to use their knowledge of the English language and context to work out the meanings.

Word	Word in context
ornery	him being so ignorant, ornery and low-down
ole	'Yo' ole father'
cowhide	He told Huck he'd cowhide him black-and-blue
doan'	'Doan' hurt me!'
lit	I lit out
low-down	Huck felt low-down

Extend by looking at the way that Jim speaks. Students could translate Jim's speech into Standard English. Or they might research the linguistic roots of Jim's African American Vernacular English by looking at some pidgins and creoles.

Other suitable **Real Reads** texts include

***Tess of the d'Urbervilles* (Hardy)**   Look at the language of Tess's mother.

RELIGIOUS CONTEXT

VALUES AND BELIEFS

Exploring the values that underpin the world's great religions can help students see that they share much common ground.

Mary Magdalene (New Testament)

Try identifying the characteristics of Mary Magdalene and Jesus. What characteristics do students admire that they might try to emulate in their own lives?

Extend by identifying the lessons being taught about how Christians should behave and treat other people. Students could identify situations from their own lives where they might exhibit these qualities.

Other suitable **Real Reads** texts include

Mahabharata: Rolling the Dice (Part 2 of the trilogy)

Siddhartha Gautama: The Life of The Buddha

Muhammad: The Life of The Prophet

SOCIAL AND HISTORICAL CONTEXT

MAKING A TIMELINE

An appreciation of the social and historical context of a story can help the reader make sense of the issues a writer is exploring. Identifying the way in which stories relate to real events can also help to engage readers who are more interested in fact than fiction.

A Tale of Two Cities (Dickens)

Try creating a timeline showing historical events mentioned in the 'Taking things further' section as well as the events in the novel.

Extend by separating the events that occur in France and in England using a map. What contrasts are there between England and France? Why did Dickens set the novel in a historical period removed from his own? What might he have been trying to show about Victorian England?

60

RESEARCH

The Time Machine (Wells)

Try finding out about Darwin's theory of evolution. Make links with Wells's story.

Extend by considering the way in which Wells uses the Morlocks and the Eloi to represent different classes in the society he knew.

Other suitable **Real Reads** texts include

Journey to the West (Cheng'en)   Find out about the Buddhist monk Xuanzang's pilgrimage and its place in Chinese folklore.

Huckleberry Finn (Twain)   Find out about slavery in the United States; in particular look at the north–south divide in the mid-1880s.

LUCAN
LIBRARY
TEL. 6216422

BIOGRAPHICAL CONTEXT

Exploring aspects of an author's life that might have provided the inspiration for writing can add a new dimension to reading, and can encourage students in their own writing.

Persuasion (Austen)

Try researching upper and middle class society in Bath and Lyme Regis at the time when the Austen family stayed there. Look at extracts from the novel to see how Jane Austen represented English Regency society.

Extend by finding out about Jane Austen's own relationship with Tom Lefroy. What feelings and experiences might have influenced the plot of this and other novels?

Other suitable **Real Reads** texts include

David Copperfield **(Dickens)** Find out about Dickens's childhood experiences and consider how they relate to those of David Copperfield.

Wuthering Heights **(Emily Brontë)** Research the district of Haworth in northern England and the moors around it, and consider why Emily Brontë used them for the setting of her novel.

PROFILING THE WRITER

Try comparing whole stories or extracts by a single author such as Jane Austen to identify common themes and ideas, characters, settings and stylistic features.

Extend by referring to extracts from the original texts.

Other suitable **Real Reads** texts include

The novels of Charles Dickens

The novels of Thomas Hardy

LITERARY CONTEXT
GENRE

Exploring the generic features of different types of novel can help students understand the evolution of the novel, and make judgements about their own preferences, encouraging independent reading.

War of the Worlds (Wells)

Try creating a mood board including representations of all of the scientific (and pseudo-scientific) motifs.

Extend by researching other science fiction stories. Students could build a timeline and explore when and why the first such novels were written. Go on to read selected passages or whole novels in the genre.

Other suitable **Real Reads** texts include

***The Murders in the Rue Morgue* (Poe)**   Find out about the early examples of detective fiction and explore possible reasons why the genre has become so popular.

***The Riddle of the Sands* (Childers)**   Find out more about early espionage novels, and talk about why the genre has remained so popular.